CELTIC SPIRITUALITY

MARIA BUCKLEY

ᘰERCIER PRESS

CONTENTS

1 The Celts   7

2 Celtic Spirituality and Beliefs   13

3 The Early Christian Church   22

4 Christianity meets Celticism   33

5 Monks, Scribes and Animals   43

6 Celtic Spirituality in Folk Culture   52

7 The Survival of Pagan Celtic
     Practices   62

8 Celtic Echoes   73

   Select Bibliography   79

1

THE CELTS

When with the coming of Christianity the Celtic Irish at last found a means of making a written record of their early history, the model they used was of a series of invasions going back to the time of Noah's flood. These are almost entirely mythical but they may well reflect a folk memory of immigration and assimilation. The oldest document about these early incursionists was the *Lebor Gabála* (*Book of Invasions*) and it lists, among others, Fomorians, giant sea-pirates who came from the islands of the north, Fir Bolg and Milesians who hailed from Spain. The name 'Fir Bolg' could disguise the Belgae, who probably made their way to the south coast through the English Channel, the Hispanic origins of the sons of Mil could well have been a euhemeristic version of an actual incursion from Iberia, and the Fomorian giants may have been a memory of early Scandinavian freebooters.

The Irish Celts, who, it is thought, settled in Ireland around 500 BC, were curious not only about their own past but about that of their predecessors on the westerly island. They sought explanations for the megalithic remains, dolmens, passage graves and tumuli (especially those that dominated the fertile basin of the Boyne), remains that they viewed with a religious awe. The special reverence and potency associated with the kingly seats of Tara in County Meath and Emain Macha near Armagh City that persisted into historical times is part of the same process.

The word 'Celts' (*Keltoi* to the Greeks and *Celtae* to the Romans) may never have been used by the people themselves. The name was applied to a nomadic and warlike people who, originating in south central Europe, spread east and west. These warriors were equipped with iron weapons and fought battles on foot and from spiked-wheeled chariots. They attacked Delphi and sacked Rome but were just as happy to fight with each other, preferring to maintain small independent tribal units. They fought naked or in linen shirts and relied on individual bravery and noise to subdue their enemies. Their Irish descendants continued to affect this armourless battle gear even against the invading Normans, who were protected by chain mail and had stirruped war horses.

The Celts' fascination with those they perceived as their own particular ancestors seems positively Shintoist. They held in their imaginations a heroic age with epic warriors and conflicts, and queens as powerful and independent as any king. This race has made such a strong impression because their characteristic artefacts, marked by rich and subtle design, are found all over Europe, but they may not have been even the largest group of finally homogeneous people who by the fifth century could be called Gaels and were to be the object of the attention of Christian missionaries. They had by then a common language: a version of *ur*-Celtic that finally became Irish, Manx and Gaelic.

In this language, they created, memorised and passed down by word of mouth marvellous tales about what they held as their past. The great prose and verse epic *Táin Bó Cuailgne*, which tells of an epic struggle over a bull between Connacht's Medb and Ulster's Conchubar and describes the death of Cú Chulainn, the greatest of the northern heroes, may have its origin in the struggle which pushed the historical Ulaid east of the Bann. Aesthetics aside, the most significant thing about the epic is that a bull is at its centre. The bull, like the Cretan minotaur, has divine qualities but is firmly rooted in the earthly. This symbolism is a good example of the Celtic tendency to combine the divine with the earthly, the Otherworld with the natural world. The great Gaels of Ireland, as Chesterton called them, may have been bonny fighters but they were fighting farmers and stockmen. They were almost pathologically independent and isolated each from the other, preferring small divisions of territory with settlements not unlike the ranch system of the early American West.

The pre-Christian society was a hierarchical one with clear class distinctions, a fine sense of aesthetic design and an unusual respect for poetry, traditional lore (including genealogy) and storytelling. The poets shared with scholars, physicians, jurists, top artificers and scholars membership of the *aes dána* ('men of art'), whose social stratum was fixed between that of nobles and free commoners. In a territory where there was no 'state', the regulation of society, punishment for crime and system of inheritance were largely the responsibility of the blood-group called the *fine*, which involved collateral as well as direct descendants and baffled even the jurists in its complexity. Relationships between classes were on a client basis, including the lowest class of the 'unfree', which numbered farm labourers, unskilled wood- and metal-workers, and captives and slaves. There was some scope for upward mobility: if a low-grade metal-worker's child developed sufficient skill, he might be accepted as a free commoner and eventually as a member of the *aes dána*.

At the core of the conservation of Celtic society and its structures were the priests or druids but we have very little information about what they believed, as opposed to their function in society. We know that they had considerable power both over individuals and over the regulation of society, and it is speculated that they may have engaged in human sacrifice. Druidic ritual was not preserved precisely because druids were the enemies of Christianity. They could not long survive the establishment of Christianity in Ireland. The druids make up one part of Celtic belief that was not handed down to us through Christianity.

2

CELTIC SPIRITUALITY AND BELIEFS

Part of the spiritual or mystical belief of the Celts was founded on their relationship with the Tuatha dé Danann ('people of the goddess Danu'), the race of people from whom the Celts had wrested hegemony over Ireland. When the Tuatha dé Danann were defeated by the Celts in the centuries before Christ, the tribe of Danu were believed no longer to exert earthly power but to have retreated to the mounds, barrows and tumuli that had existed for thousands of years. From these places they exerted their dominion over the Otherworld only, being called the fairies or 'good people' but sometimes interfering with or accepting a visit from a human king or warrior.

The god Dagda seems also to have been a Tuatha dé Danann god adopted by the Celts.

He mated with various territorial goddessses, including Boann, the goddess of the Rive Boyne. They had a son called Oengus, whose palace, the Celts believed, was Newgrange.

Most of the divinities worshipped by the Celts were not specific to any one area of life. Goddesses were spirits of places, rivers, wells and hills; gods were warriors, craftsmen and prophets. Archaeologist and historian Liam de Paor observes:

> It is rather as if the pagan Irish lived and breathed with one foot in this world and one foot in the Otherworld; the two worlds interpenetrated. Most of what we can guess about pre-Christian Ireland suggests a tissue of magical practices and rituals, the observation of omens, the use of spells and incantatory formulas and the avoidance of unlucky actions.

For the Celts, the king, whether the local lord or the ruler of a province, occupied a sacred position, propitiating the gods and the elements to protect his people from the forces of nature, such as drought, famine and disease, and from the arbitrary displeasure of the deities. The king was seen as the mate of the goddess of place – that is, married to his territory and his people. The ceremony in which the king assumed sovereignty and mated with the goddess, symbolically or otherwise, was called a *feis*, and this was a ceremony that conferred legitimacy on the king's reign. For instance, the king of Tara, a place of special mythic significance, mated with the goddess Medb Lethderg.

It may well have been the case that an actual mating took place at the time of the inauguration of the king. In the twelfth century, Gerald of Wales reports having heard a story of a northern king mating publicly with a white mare on the occasion of his inauguration, the mare symbolising the territory to be ruled by the king. The mare was then killed, cut up and boiled. As part of the ceremony, the pieces of meat were eaten by the assembled people and the king bathed in the broth in which the meat had been boiled.

For these people, whether pagan or Christian, the concept of justice was crucial, and this is evident in the early literature. If a king's reign is just, peace and prosperity will follow; if not, there will be conflict, famine, pestilence and all manner of disasters. The Fir Bolg, who preceded the Tuatha dé Danann, who in turn preceded the Celts, were the first to introduce the idea of sacral kingship. Of one of their kings, Eochaidh Mac Eirc, it was said:

> No rain fell during his reign, but only the dew; there was no year without harvest. Falsehood was banished from Ireland during his time, and he it was who first established the rule of justice there.'

In the Leinster saga 'The Destruction of Da Dearga's Hostel', the King of Ireland, Conaire, is slain. The story relates that during Conaire's reign the country was peaceful and prosperous:

> So great was the harmony that existed that no man slew another in Ireland in his reign, and to every man the voice of his fellow was sweet as harpstrings. No wind tossed the hair of cows from the middle of spring to the middle of autumn. His reign was not thundery or stormy.

Conversely, during the reign in Tara of an unjust king:

> For a year after that he was in kingship in Tara and no grass came through the ground, nor leaf through trees, nor grain into corn. Then the men of Ireland rejected him from his kingship because he was a false prince.

The society which the Christian missionaries found was not unaware of religion. It had its gods and goddesses who lived in the Otherworld, a kind of idealised life on earth where all appetites were satisfied. This was the pagan Celtic heaven; the Celts did not believe in hell. The dead went to a place variously called Hy Breasail, Tír na nÓg ('the Land of Youth'), Magh Meala ('the Honey Plain'), the Gentle Land or Magh Dá Cheo ('the Plain of Two Fogs') In his Introduction to *Irish Sagas*, Myles Dillon describes this Otherworld :

> The Irish Underworld is a country where there is no sickness nor age nor death;

where happiness lasts for ever, food and drink do not diminish when consumed, to wish for something is to possess it; where a hundred years are as one day. This Land of the Living is in the Western Sea. A beautiful girl approaches the hero and sings to him of this happy island. He follows her and they sail away in a boat of glass and are seen no more. Or else he returns after three days to find that he has been away for 300 years. Sometimes it is a castle in which the hero has some strange adventures, and then the castle vanishes, and he finds himsllf alone again.

The best-known story of this kind concerns the Fianna warrior, Oisín, the son of Fianna leader Fionn Mac Cumhail. One day Oisín is beguiled by a beautiful young woman, Niamh Cinn Óir – Niamh of the Golden Hair – into leaving Ireland and going to her country with her on her snow-white steed – to Tír na nÓg, 'the Land of Youth'.

Oisín spends three years there with his princess but, although his every wish is satisfied in this land of perfect happiness, he misses his home and wonders how his fellow Fianna warriors are faring. Niamh lends him her white horse to return to Ireland but warns him that if he sets foot on Irish soil he will never see her again. Oisín agrees to this condition, but when he returns to Ireland he finds that the Fianna and their exploits are just a memory of a heroic age. He has been absent for 300 years. Real time in nature is eternal time in Tír na nÓg. When he inadvertantly puts a foot on the ground in an attempt to help some Irish weaklings to move a rock, he is turned into an old man, his horse flying for home. This story dovetails nicely into Christianity: St Patrick comes to baptise Oisín before he dies.

In a similar story, written down in the eighth century, a warrior called Bran sets out in search of the Otherworld promised to him by a magical woman. When he returns to the natural world of Ireland and tells the people on the shore, 'I am Bran son of Febal', their mystified reponse is: 'We know him not but the Voyage of Bran is one of our ancient stories.'

It is evident from their literature that the

Celts also believed in reincarnation or trans-migration of souls. In her book *Irish Folklore*, Bríd Mahon describes:

> the story of the hero who dies dishonoured
> and is reborn many times – as a salmon,
> a stag, a hound and a great boar roaming
> the forest – until his final reincarnation
> as a man, when he redeems himself and
> is restored to favour among the gods.

It is clear that this story has its roots in the Indo-European tradition and it reminds a contemporary reader of the Hindu belief in reincarnation. But it is also the case that this kind of belief in ultimate redemption and a hero 'being restored to favour among the gods' could be integrated, without too much shaping, into a Christian monotheistic religion.

In his *Celtic Mythology*, Pronsias Mac Cana described shape-shifting – heroes taking the form of one or more animals – and has this to say about the general Celtic concept of an afterlife:

the Celtic idea of the Otherworld, as this is realised in the literature, allowed remarkable imaginative fluidity, with the natural and supernatural seeming continually to merge and commingle in an almost free variation.

The stories about Fionn and the Fianna, collectively known as the *Fiannaíocht*, emphasise both the closeness of the warriors to nature and their freedom of movement between the natural and supernatural worlds.

We know also that the voyage to the happy Otherworld was a popular theme among Christian monastic scribes.

3

THE EARLY CHRISTIAN CHURCH

The story of Patrick has been the source of much piety and considerably more controversy but at least he has left documents, the most reassuring thing you can offer an historian. *Confessio* and *Epistola ad Milites Corotici* establish him as a real person from whom it is possible to shake the accretion of the hagiography of later ages.

The *Confession* describes Patrick's capture, his six-year captivity in either Antrim or Mayo, depending on your chauvinism, his escape and his dream in which 'a man called Victor' gave him 'many letters' from the Irish begging him: '*ut venias et adhuc ambulas inter nos*' ('come and walk among us again'). This short book really provides little information, apart from the fact that Patrick was, as he said, but an unpolished

Latinist, together with unidentifiable place names (his home, *Bannavem Taberniae* and *Silva Vocluti*, the place of his captivity) and his steadfast belief in the faith that he brought from his own Romanised country. The *Letter to Coroticus's Soldiers* is full of stern rebuke of those men of a so-called Christian prince who killed Irish converts.

The faith that Patrick brought was parochial and episcopal, but as it turned out, monasticism suited the Irish better both socially and psychologically. The eremetic tradition struck an answering note in the Gaelic temperament, in spite of, or because of, the obvious sensuality of their culture. The episcopal system depended on metropolitans – bishops who presided over a province of lesser prelates – and this implied the existence of some kind of urban centre. Such did not exist in Ireland until the Norsemen established them in Dublin, Waterford and Limerick. The only settlements before that were accretions to the monastic sites. This lack of metropolises, as much as the place's legendary reputation, may have been the reason for Patrick's selection of Emain Macha as the centre of his mainly northern establishment (if indeed it was he who chose it). Emain Macha was at least an identifiable centre.

The slow Christianisation of Ireland and the assimilation of Brehon laws and Druidic lore seem to have been achieved without bloodshed. They were accomplished, however, in a small country where internecine conflict, though ritualised, was endemic. One reason for the growth of a monastic structure may be that the grouping of individual huts within a stockade replicated the characteristically isolated Celtic settlements. In some cases the new groupings grew large, forming what were in fact university campuses that in time attracted students from the various British kingdoms and from Gaul. A foundation such as Clonmacnoise might have passed for a village because of its population of religious, students and those providing ancillary services.

It was as if with the coming of the monks the *tuath* had found an intellectual, social and administrative centre; the monastic settlement could well contain its prison, hospital and church, and its abbot was the spiritual equivalent of the *rí*. From the tenth century onwards the enclosures would have contained the characteristic free-standing bell tower, which, with its impregnable walls, door set high above ground level and conical top, became the characteristic Irish icon. Many compounds would have cross-slabs and, later on, high crosses which acted as a kind of pictorial bible.

The Celtic family group, the *fine*, was close-knit but not nuclear. It gave a man a sense of familial association that bridged five generations and inculcated a sense of very local patriotism. (The women had membership of the *fine* by marriage or blood connection.) It also meant that separation from the unit was in effect an exile. This was the origin of the phrase 'white martyrdom' that was voluntarily undertaken by some of the more austere monks: 'when he gives up all that is dear to him for God's sake'. The stories of Irish monks standing up to their necks in ice-cold water seem less unlikely when one considers the monastic remains on Sceilg Mhíchil off the Kerry coast. But even there St Fíonán was in Irish territory and on the rare days of fair weather the green homeland could be seen. A much greater martyrdom was to leave Ireland

and go to Britain or Europe as a '*perigrinator pro Christo* ('exile for Christ')'.

Patrick, although not a monk himself (though there is a tradition that he lived as one for a period), is credited with extreme self-mortification, spending a biblical forty days on a tiny island in Lough Derg in County Donegal and a further forty on top of Croagh Patrick in County Mayo wresting promises from heaven for his beloved Irish. These literally purgatorial traditions have held fast for 1,500 years, providing a pair of medieval pilgrimages that have now lasted into the third millennium of Christian belief.

Monasticism had begun in the Church with the 'desert fathers', who took Christ's counsels of perfection literally. A typical eremite was St Antony (251-356), who lived in the Egyptian desert and spent his time in prayer, study and necessary manual work. In time he was joined by disciples, upon whom he imposed a simple rule. The idea of a community came from such small beginnings, although Antony, at the age of about sixty, left the community to live alone again in a cave in northern Egypt for his remaining forty years. The coenobitic (literally 'community living') movement spread east and west and came to Ireland partly from Wales, in the persons of Finnian of Clonard, Aidan of Ferns, Senan of Scattery Island (near Kilrush, County Clare) and Brendan of Clonfert, who had been trained by Illtyd of Caldey and Wales's patron saint, David of Mynyw. It also came partly from Scotland, from the famous *Candida Casa* of St Ninian on the coast of Galloway, near modern Stranraer. In Ireland, the northern founders included Enda of Aran, who is credited with the establishment of the first Irish monastery and the imposition of the extreme ascetic rule, Tighernagh of Clones, Coirpre of Coleraine and, most significant, Finnian of Movilla, who was Colum Cille's tutor.

It was customary for each monk to have his own cell, though there were exceptions, with the abbot, who was most likely in holy orders, occupying one that was slightly larger and set at a distance from the others. The cells were made of wood or of the staple Celtic material of wattle and daub and have long since disappeared. The Irish 'desert fathers', however, took to western coasts and islands where there were no trees and made their 'beehive' cells of stone, which may still be seen, notably in Sceilg Mhíchil off the south coast of Kerry and on the Dingle Peninsula, also in County Kerry.

In the 'golden age' of peaceful monasticism, the monastery palisade would have enclosed, among other buildings, a scriptorium, where the scriptures were copied and the illuminated manuscripts that were the glory of Christian Ireland's first millennium were created. The monks wore tunics covered by a hooded woollen robe called a *casula* and their tonsure consisted of shaving the front of the scalp up to the crown of the head. Manual labour was an important part of the day, which was long and broken by no more than two meals, largely vegetarian. Lent, Advent and the forty days after Pentecost were times of great austerity, while Wednesdays and Fridays were days of special mortification.

One notable characteristic of Irish monasticism was that the monks did not belong to a particular order: there was no mother house and no abbot-general. Variations in rule were common, depending upon the decision of the local abbot.

The rule devised by Columban was exemplarily severe and sprang most likely from the austerity he had experienced during his novitiate in Bangor under Comgall. His insistence upon it and on Irish practices brought him into controversy with Pope Gregory.

Though the main study of the monks was the sacred books and commentaries, profane literature began to flourish as well. The Celts, like the Norsemen who tried to destroy their civilisation, were illiterate. Apart from a primitive alphabetical system of grooves on the edges of stones called *ogham* which sufficed for sepulchral memorials, they had no means of rendering their vast store of knowledge. The lore of the *aes dána*, the cultured class, had been preserved in prodigious feats of memorising, and this habit persisted long after the coming of writing. The complicated Brehon laws and the hero stories of the Gaels had replaced written history. Memory is not precise and is as creative as other aspects of the imagination.

The coming of Latin uncial provided a means of recording this vernacular culture and the great hero cycles, which told of such demigods as Medb, Cú Chulainn, Deirdre, Fionn and the Red Branch Knights, were finally written down and formalised. The island's half-remembered, half-imagined early history, its laws, traditions and religious beliefs, were recorded in a series of great books which have preserved what was understood about Ireland and its past by contemporaries from the coming of Christianity up to the time of the Tudor destruction of the Gaelic civilisation. A tradition of poetry flourished, appearing first as idle doodles on the margins of religious manuscripts. Its main themes were God and nature, flora and fauna, the year's turning – all characteristic of a people which lived as much as possible out of doors – but ribaldry, wit and delight in the grotesque played their parts too.

The old monks also helped to preserve a delight in the works of classical antiquity and they played their parts in the re-education of a Europe that had grown dark with barbarian intrusion. Colum Cille and Columban were only the first and most famous of a series of religious who brought not only sacred knowledge but liberal learning to the continent. Alcuin, who was trained by Irish monks in Northumbria, became Charlemagne's minister of education and one of the greatest preservers and advancers of the humanities in the middle ages. Sedulius Scottus (*c.*820–*c.*880) and Johannes Scotus Eriugena (*c.*810–*c.*870), both labelled Irish, the latter twice over, lead the list of *docti* who were the glory of pre-Renaissance Europe and who gave their homeland the justifiable title of a land of scholars.

The period from the acceptance of Christianity until the first coming of the Vikings is usually regarded as a golden age, though the country was still as vulnerable to the twin visitations of famine and pestilence as it had been in the fifth century. Struggles between rival dynasties continued, often with clerics in the opposing armies. There is a strong tradition that even so saintly a man as Colum Cille was sufficiently susceptible to his position as a noble member of the Cenél Conaill to have taken part in the battle of Cúl Dreimhne as a prelude to his leaving Ireland to found the great monastery of Iona. The battle was fought against the Connachta, in around 562, appropriately enough under Ben Bulben, a groyne that separates Connacht from Ulster both geographically and mythically.

Still the monasteries continued to flourish, combining aesthetics with worship. It was the period of the great *Book of Kells* (made in Iona and brought home to Meath to save it from the Norse marauders), the Ardagh Chalice, the Athlone crucifixion plaque, the high crosses and the other glories of Irish art. It was also a period of the preservation and growth of learning recorded in beautifully written and sumptuously produced books.

By the time the first Scandinavian pirates appeared off Lindisfarne, Iona and Rathlin in the last decade of the eighth century, there had been a tradition of love of learning, appreciation of beauty and delight in the chronicling of romance and high deeds for nearly a millennium. The natural inclinations of the people had been enhanced by the Christian missionaries and Ireland shone like a beacon of faith and learning in an umbrous Europe.

4

CHRISTIANITY MEETS CELTICISM

There exists in various manuscript forms a long twelfth-century compilation called *Agallamh na Seanórach* (*The Colloquy of the Ancients*). It looks back to the early days of Christianity and seeks to construct a bridge between the pagan Celtic and the Christian. In it St Patrick talks to the remaining members of the Fianna, including Oisín and the other great warrior, Caoilte (all now ancient). The pagan Fianna tell him about their way of life and introduce him to the lore (*dinnseanchas*) of the hills, forests and rivers of the beloved homeland that they, as roaming hunters, know intimately.

When Patrick asks what kind of man Fionn himself was, Caoilte gives him the justifiably famous – and lyrical – answer: 'Were but the brown leaf which the wood sheds from it gold

– were but the white billows silver – Fionn would have given it all away.' Caoilte continues in answer to Patrick to explain the moral code by which the Fianna lived so generously and well: *Glaine inár gcroí, neart inár ngéag, beart de réir ár mbriathar* ('Honesty in our hearts, strength in our limbs and deeds to honour our promises'). Patrick on several occasions expresses his approval of the stories he is hearing by saying: 'May victory and blessing attend you.'

It is clear that the monkish writer of this text has convinced himself that the values of the pagan culture of the Fianna are in themselves 'Christian' and that there is no tension or conflict between the two codes of living. This is proven when Patrick, who expresses unease about spending so much time in listening to stories at the expense of prayer and contemplation, is reassured the next morning by the visit of two guardian angels, who say to him:

> Beloved holy cleric, those ancient warriors can tell you no more than a third of their stories, by reason of forgetfulness and lack of memory. And see to it that what

they say be written on poets' staves and in learned men's words, for it will be a delight to gatherings of people and to noblemen in later times to listen to those tales.

There are passages of great lyric beauty in *Agallamh na Seanórach*, for instance Caoilte's words to Patrick as they stand together in the Fews Mountains in County Armagh on a snowy night:

Winter is cold; the wind has risen; the fierce stark-wild stag arises; not warm tonight is the unbroken mountain, even though the swift stag be belling.

Writing about the Táin, David Greene in his essay on 'Táin Bó Cuailgne', in *Irish Sagas*, remarks:

But in no country did the Church make its peace with the old learning as quickly or as thoroughly as in Ireland: the elegiac poem in the old bardic style on St Columba, who died in 597, is sufficient

proof that a complete understanding had
been arrived at by that date.

Writing in Ireland was little known before the
fifth century, and writing in Irish not until the
seventh century. Perhaps the fact that the *Táin*
was first written down in the seventh century
suggests that by then paganism had sufficiently
faded into the background that the heroic tales,
with all their ritual violence, had become
respectable.

When Patrick and the other missionaries
brought Christianity to Ireland, the Celtic Irish
must have recognised it in a belief not all that
alien to them. The people hold that death was
the end only of the body and that a life of the
spirit continued in another place. Their worship
of the sun and the spirits of rivers and lakes
indicated a pleasure in the natural world and
this characterised their vernacular poetry when
they found the means to write it down. They
made their ancestors into heroes and their heroes
into gods. They took to Christianity in time and
subtly altered its practice to suit their temper-
aments. Their attitude to life, in so far as we can
judge it, was on the whole honourable, cheerful

and sensual. Divorce was prevalent and the practice of polygamy among the noble class persisted until Tudor times. In general their theology was wary but not fearful. The coming of Christianity made changes but assimilation even in this continued to be characteristic. The Gaelic way of life, modified and sensitised by the adopted faith, survived the Norman invasion and persisted in three-quarters of the country until the end of the sixteenth century. We feel that influence still: as Sean O'Faolain put it in his superlative monograph *The Irish* (1947), it has given us:

'that old atavistic individualism which tends to make all Irishmen inclined to respect no laws at all; and though this may be socially deplorable it is humanly admirable, and makes life much more tolerable and charitable and easy-going and entertaining.

It is interesting to speculate why pagan Celtic Ireland took so readily and with such apparent lack of bloodshed to the new faith of Christianity.

In his book *Early Celtic Christianity*, Brendan Lehane expresses the view that:

> the answer must lie in two phenomena. One was the refined variety of the new religion that reached Ireland – the monastic form from Wales and Gaul. The other was – must have been – the character of the Irish.

and that:

> For the glories of God's kingdom were to be achieved through an ascetic strictness – an obedience to precise rules – rare on the Continent; yet the journey was fringed with unimaginable beauty and poetic delights. It is a polarity that lies behind the energy, endurance and persistent humour that pervades the character of archetypal Irish Christians.

Learning also endeared Christianity to the Irish. They had their hero tales, their tales of kings and gods; now they had all the stories of the

Bible, some plausible, some fantastic, and all the theology of Christianity to get their teeth into. They already had the concept of triads – tricephalic heads such as a famous head in siliceous sandstone from first-century Cavan have survived – and it is said that St Patrick taught the very receptive audience of Irish people the meaning of the Trinity by using a shamrock.

St Patrick's method of Christianising Ireland was one that has been called 'inculturation' by John Walsh and Thomas Bradley in their *A History of the Irish Church 400–700 AD*:

> that is, wherever possible he would have attempted to adopt the cherished religious values and practices of the Celts to Christianity. However, he would seem to have made no effort to accommodate certain of their approaches. Oak groves, sacred wells and some festivals were easily incorporated into the new religion and the new clergy were soon to find a privileged position as members of the *aes dana,* but obnoxious cults like the worship

'of idols and things impure [*Confesio*, 41], sun-worship, the sucking of another's nipples as a sign of friendship and the eating of food offered to false gods' were repugnant to him and he made every effort to stamp them out. Later tradition highlights his conflicts with the druids.

St Patrick was said to have had dramatic confrontations with pagans in the early part of his mission to Ireland but these tales may owe little to reality and more to the desire to make a Biblical – Moses-like – hero of him. He lit the first Paschal fire on the Hill of Slane, defying a ban placed by the then all-powerful druids on all fires because one of their own festivals was to take place the next day. He is also said to have caused the death of a king's magician who insulted him and his religion. Patrick was, according to the evidence of his own writings and the writings of others, concerned to extirpate the sun-worship practised by the Celts. When Etna Alba, a Celtic princess, asks Patrick:

Who is God?...Where is his dwelling?... In the seas, in the rivers, in the mountains, in the valleys?

he replies:

Our God, God of all men, God of heaven
      and earth, seas and rivers,
God of sun and moon, of all the stars,
God of high mountains and of lowly valleys,
God over heaven, and in heaven, and
      under heaven.
He has a dwelling in heaven and earth
      and sea,
and in all things that are in them.
He inspires all things, He quickens all
      things,
He is over all things, He supports all
      things . . .

Likewise, 'The Deer's Cry', a poem attributed to Saint Patrick but no more likely to have been written by him than the famous 'St Patrick's Breastplate', emphasises the omnipresence of God. There is no dualism, no division between the natural world and the heavens, between body and soul:

I arise today
Through the strength of heaven:
Light of sun,
Radiance of moon,
Splendour of fire,
Speed of lightning,
Swiftness of wind,
Depth of sea,
Stability of earth,
Firmness of rock.

(version Meyer)

There is an exquisitely beautiful 'prayer' from the eighth century which also succinctly and lyrically conveys the idea of the omnipresent God:

Be thou my vision, O Lord of my heart,
Nought is all else to me save that Thou
     art,
Thou my best thought in the day and the
     night,
Waking or sleeping, Thy presence my
     light.

(version Hull)

5

MONKS, SCRIBES AND ANIMALS

Although early Irish Christianity was predominantly monastic and ascetic, this severe regimen was saved from inhumanity by a delight in nature, by the sense of humour frequently manifested by the monks and scribes, and by the fondness for animals shown by many monks, according to the stories that were written down about them.

Hospitality was the first rule of the monastery, as it was of palace, castle and ordinary home in Celtic-Christian Ireland. Monasteries were open to all: travellers, the sick and the poor.

Animal connections abound in the stories of the early Irish Church. A flock of singing birds was said to have welcomed Patrick when he returned to Ireland on his mission of evangelisation. Later on, animals befriended monks, provided company for them in their monastic loneliness and helped them in practical ways. From their dealings with the animals, the monks could formulate lessons applicable to their human disciples, as in the following story about an early Christian saint, Ciaran of Ossory. A wild boar helps him to build his cell: 'And that boar was Ciaran's first disciple and served him like a monk in that place.' Four other animals come from the wild to live with Ciaran: a fox, a badge, a wolf and a stag. 'And they abode with him as tame as could be.' When the fox turns wild again, stealing Ciaran's goatskin slippers to eat them, Ciaran sends the badger to bring him back. He remonstrates with the fox, although mildly: 'Behold our water is sweet and common to all, and our food likewise is distributed in common among us all.' The fox repents, does penance fasting and returns to the fold: 'He abode with the rest in familiar converse.'

Another St Ciaran, St Ciaran of Clonmacnoise, had a favourite dun cow, and when she died the monks of his monastery preserved her hide as a relic. The famous St Kevin of Glendalough loved all the beasts of the field and the birds of the air and it is related that one day, while he stood with his arms outstretched in prayer, a raven nested on his arm. Out of respect to the raven, he did not move until she had laid her eggs. There is also a charming story about one of the many Saint Mochuas of the early Christian Church. It is said that he had a cock, a mouse and a fly to help him in his observance of his religious duties and his reading of the psalms.

There are many other such stories of animals helping the monks, or of animals – deer, a dove – being used by divine providence to indicate to the monks where a new monastic foundation should be established. It is clear from all these stories that the monks were gentle, courteous and generous to their animal companions, regarding them as helpers or, in their innocence and trustfulness, as emissaries from God. One of the many miracles attributed to Saint Brigid in *Cogitosus's Life of Saint Brigid the Virgin* is that she fed a hungry dog from her pot of boiling pork but her guests found that the amount of food remaining was 'still undiminished'. Brigid is able to benefit from a very loving, reciprocal relationship with various animals, domestic and wild: she gets three times the normal quantity of milk from her cow by milking her three times in one day; a wild boar settles down calmly with her herd of pigs. Brigid's story is a notable example of Christian saints disappearing under a patchwork of old stories about the pagan divinities who came before them. Although Brigid seems to have been a historical abbess who founded a monastery in Kildare, her hagiography reveals her image to have been that of a pagan goddess or goddesses of the same name.

Although the devotion of the monks and the labour of the scribes tended exclusively towards Christian subjects, in time a native style of lyric nature poetry developed, in the shade of Christianity, as it were. This was a linear descendent of the Celtic love for – even worship of – the natural and the wild. Monks who were copying sacred manuscripts doodled in the margins and in time this marginalia devloped from scribbling to the earliest lyric poetry in Ireland. For the scribe, like the ascetic monk, nature brought companionship and solace:

A hedge of trees surrounds me,
A blackbird's lay sings to me;
Above my lined booklet
The trilling birds chant to me.
In a grey mantle from the top of the
  bushes
The cuckoo sings;
Verily – may the Lord shield me!
Well do I write under the greenwood
  tree.

(*version* Meyer)

The scribe who wrote the following lines has a
sense of proportion about himself. Rueful and
self-mocking, he still has a sense of a power
greater than himself that moves the pen when
he is too tired to do so. The translation by Kuno
Meyer conveys a great lyrical energy, particularly
in the last two lines:

My hand is weary with writing,
My sharp quill is not steady,
My slender-beaked pen pours forth
A black draught of shining dark-blue
  ink.

A more famous example of the humour of the scribe is the poem 'The Monk and His Cat', which was translated by Robin Flower and which is often better known by the cat's name, Pangur Bán. The writer compares himself, gently and humorously, to his white cat:

> Hunting mice is his delight
> Hunting words I sit all night.

In *Early Celtic Christianity*, Denis Lehane remarks that it was greatly to the advantage of the Celtic Irish that they had never been colonised by the Romans and that, although they adopted Latin for the purposes of devotion and scripture, they were free to develop a literature – the oldest surviving literature in Europe – in the vernacular.

The tension between the Celtic version of Christianity and the Roman, episcopal version which was oberved in the rest of Europe and in England culminated with the Synod of Whitby in 664. The ostensible reason for the synod was to harmonise the method of calculating the date of Easter, which is the great movable feast of the Christian calendar. The Irish stubbornly held to their own dating system, which gave them a date earlier than the European, and anomalies arose; for instance in the Northumbrian court, the king, who had been converted by Irish missionaries, observed Easter, while his queen, who had English (Roman) religious instructors, was still undergoing the penitential rites of Lent.

The other areas of contention were the low status of bishops in the Celtic Church, which was still largely monastic and abbatial, and the apparently superficial but vexed question of the tonsure. It is thought that the Irish either shaved their heads from ear to ear along the vertical plane, leaving the hair long at the back of the neck, or shaved a cross on their heads, leaving four tufts of hair to stick out. Those who took instruction directly from Rome favoured the more conventional circular tonsure with a fringe of hair all around. This difference gave the Roman adherents a stick with which to beat the Irish. The Celtic tonsure was a pagan practice, they alleged, with its roots in druidic religion. Others said it harked back to the appearance of Judas Iscariot.

The Irish Church, in short, wanted to go its

own way and resisted being made to conform to
regulations in a homogeneous Roman ecclesi-
astical empire. The Celtic elements in its make-
up, some of which it had assimilated from the
pagan pre-Christian way of life, distinguished it
from the other Christian churches.

At Whitby, the Irish lost. The synod came
down firmly in favour of Roman customs.
Naturally some monk wrote a poem about this
subject too. In the ninth century, a nameless
scribe committed the following words to his
vellum:

> To go to Rome –
> Is little profit, endless pain.
> The Master you seek in Rome
> You find at home or seek in vain.
>
> (*version* Meyer)

In general the transition from paganism to
Christianity was smooth and free of bloodshed.
But it was only a partial transition. In many
aspects of religious observance, especially those
connected with the seasons or with sacred places,
Christianity was merely grafted on to earlier,

Celtic pagan beliefs and practices. Many of these pagan-Christian rites persisted until the second half of the twentieth century. In one generation, the advent of television and widespread use of the motor car brought about changes in religious practices and in the underlying mindset that St Patrick and all the monks who followed him, successive waves of Viking and Norman invasion, Cromwell and the Penal Laws (to mention only some of the agents of change involved) had not succeeded in changing. How some of these beliefs manifested themselves in folk culture is the subject of the next chapter of this book.

6

CELTIC SPIRITUALITY
IN FOLK CULTURE

Some historical experts have expressed the opinion that, until the middle of the nineteenth century, Irish Catholicism, though it had long since come under the direct authority of Rome, was essentially pagan. Despite the economic disadvantages suffered by Catholics under what was effectively apartheid legislation (popularly known as the Penal Laws) in the intolerant eighteenth century, relatively few of them abandoned their traditional religion. For the peasants of the Western seaboard and the poor counties of the west and north, there was little encouragement for them to do so; nor was any concerted attempt made by the government or other agencies to encourage wholesale conversion to the Protestant religion.

Commentators at the beginning of the nineteenth century observed a peasant population
that, though wretchedly poor, even by the
standards of the day, managed to remain healthy
and cheerful. There was a great deal of merriment
and song, Mr and Mrs Hall noted during their
tour of Ireland, and indeed, for people who
depended almost completely on the potato for
sustenance, there was little enough agricultural
work to do during the long, wet and dark winter
months. Young people courted, married early
and had large families, with little thought for
the future.

The Great Famine of 1845–53 marked an
enormous change in the religious attitudes of
the Irish people, as in so many areas of Irish life.
Whereas up to this, something of the Celtic
delight in the natural world and in fleshly things
had held sway, after the Famine, the institutional
Church became increasingly repressive and
narrow. Devotionalism increased among the
remaining population, perhaps as a consequence
of the horrors the survivors had escaped during
the dark days of '47 and after. It was not only,
as some Unionists and others would have it,

after the establishment of the independent Irish state that Rome rule held sway. Long before independence, it was in the interest of the ruling British government to buttress the power of the hierarchy, which was a force for moderation, even conservatism, in political and economic life. Irish Catholicism after the Famine was profoundly hierarchical, by nature as well as by name, whereas Celtic Christianity was constructed around the smaller units of the *tuath*. Churchmen like Dublin's Cardinal Paul Cullen exerted a huge moral and social influence on their flock and on the government of the country.

In his *Short History of Ireland*, Sean McMahon comments:

> It would have been strange if the Church had not capitalised on the shock of the Biblical catastrophe, playing up a sense of visitation by a rampant Jehovah as a punishment for sin. The fact that he was very selective in his doom did not matter, since it was difficult for the inhabitants of one part of a country to have information about places even a score of miles

away. The effect was to create a docile laity for a clergy that were entering upon their period of greatest power and influence. Most of the priests were Maynooth-trained and the tenor of its practice reflected the views of a very strict, supposedly Jansenistic teaching staff. The sense of unworthiness, of the extreme difficulty of the ordinary mortal's ever being able to merit grace, made reception of the sacraments a rare event, and even children were regarded as sinners. The sense of guilt that pastors encouraged their flocks to feel was not dishonest; they felt it too, and the sins that were the most dreaded and most shocking were those concerning sex.

In such an atmosphere, lay people became increasingly estranged from their pastors, whom they treated with obsequious, even slavish respect – although this did not prevent them from mocking clerical pretensions from the safety of anonymous ballads and stories. Even until the middle years of the twentieth century, the criticism or ire of the parish priest was dreaded.

Nowhere was this repression more evident than in the area of sexual morality. The oral tradition in Irish and in the English of those people, the vernacular of whose parents or grandparents had been Irish, was frank, even earthy. *The Tailor and Ansty* is a fine example of this tradition. Eric Cross, who listened to the talk of Tailor Buckley and his wife Anastasia over countless days and nights in Gougane Barra in west Cork, summed up their gifts:

> Against a background of poverty, of severe physical handicap and pain, we were shown – had we eyes to see it – that life could be, and was, lived with an enormous appetite, gusto, gaiety, courage, and a certainty which made hay of the various religious, philosophical and political labels with which we buttressed ourselves against the real in our individual lives.
>
> We were, in fact, privileged to participate in the lives of two people, near to the end of their lives, who had preserved still the innocence, the zest, the wonder and the faults of children.

When *The Tailor and Ansty* was banned by the Irish Censorhip Board as being 'in its general tendency indecent' – surely one of the lowest points in recent Irish history – the Tailor gamely composed a new final verse to a favourite ditty of his, 'The Buttermilk Lasses'. It went:

Now all you young maidens,
Don't listen to me
For I will incite you to immoralitee
Or unnatural vice or in similar way
Corrupt or deprave you or lead you astray.

But the consequences of the decision of the Censorship Board were real and heartbreaking, as Frank O'Connor describes in his introduction to the 1964 edition of the book:

But the Tailor and Ansty had to live through it all. To all intents and purposes they were boycotted. Each week, Guard Hoare, an old friend of theirs, cycled out to see them from Ballingeary – a warning to hooligans. One afternoon three priests appeared and forced the old man on to

> his knees on his own hearth and made
> him burn his copy of the book – 'eight
> and sixpence worth', as Ansty said to me.
> To her, eight and sixpence was an awful
> lot of money.

Here the tradition, the Celtic way of seeing and living life, fell victim to the clericalism of the Irish state. Other traditions, like that of hospitality, which was so strong in ancient Ireland, also risked falling victim to a kind of exclusive clerical bigotry. Hospitality was one of the qualities of a great king or ruler and a quality valued too among the ordinary people. The rules of hospitality demanded that a visitor should always be given the best food in the house: *nua gacha bí agus seana gacha dí* (the freshest of food, the most aged drink). The law of charity, so dear to Christianity, found fertile ground on which to graft itself with the coming of Christianity to Ireland.

The great folklorist Kevin Danaher collected stories from around his own area of west Limerick that were told at the fireside by elderly people, as such stories had been told for

hundreds, even thousands, of years. A Mrs Kate
Ahern told the story of a 'poor woman going the
road one time, and she had two children along
with her and no sign of a husband.' But the
tradition of hospitality was so strong in the rural
community of the time that she would never be
refused food or shelter in any house at which she
called. Until a cleric intervenes, that is:

> But there was a certain parish priest and
> he was a very strict and hard man. And
> he thought that his woman was leading
> a bad life, and he spoke against her,
> telling his parishioners not to have any-
> thing to do with her.

But one farmer defies the priest on Christmas
Eve (his wife, being more timid and more
compliant, begins to cry when she is faced with
the dilemma):

> Parish priest or no parish priest, it will
> never be said that a poor woman and her
> children were turned from my door on
> the very night that that other poor Woman
> was refused a lodging in Bethlehem.

This story has a happy ending, in which the parish priest, having been shown a miraculous sign, repents of his hardness of heart and preaches a sermon in which he admits that he was at fault.

Still, the best approach to maintaining a semblance of Celtic paganism in the midst of devotional Roman Catholicism would seem to be that recounted by Éamon Kelly in his comic but realistic accounts of rural Irish society in the first half of the twentieth century:

> The old clergy had authority. Apart from a fondness for money you couldn't see any fault in their way of living. And if there was any fault the people'd gloss it over with, 'Don't do as they do but do as they say!'
>
> If we were to do everything they said that time, Ireland would be an open-air monastery! Small children would nearly have to be imported, for the young people'd never get the hang of things. Father Mac with a big blackthorn belting the courting couples out of the bushes

and he had the full support and the sympathy of the people in that. The mothers anyway. 'My poor man. All the trouble that young crowd are putting him to. He's worn off the bones by 'em.' Of course, to my mind there'd never be any religion in this country only for the women. The men never took to it in the same way! The women driving 'em out to Confession, up to the altar and down on their knees to say the Rosary. Timeen Sweeney, his mind a thousand miles away, doing eleven Hail Marys to the decade and twelve to the decade, and his wife saying, 'Glory, Tim!' That was like a hul-a-hul or tally-ho to him; he'd then do thirteen to the decade!

7

THE SURVIVAL
OF PAGAN CELTIC PRACTICES

Many rural societies disregarded the strictures of the clergy and continued to observe rounds or pattern days or visit holy wells that had their origin in pagan rituals or worship. A famous place of worship in County Kerry was the 'City' or Cathair Crobhdhearg in Shrone, near Rathmore. This monument, situated at the foot of the Paps, Dhá Chích Dannan ('the Breasts of the Goddess Danu or Anu') and now partly destroyed, comprised a circular wall, ten feet high and six feet thick. Inside the walls there were also a large stone circle with traces of ogham writing and a holy well. It is thought that the City was a place of worship in pre-Christian Celtic times. It has been associated with human sacrifice, as witnessed by the names of nearby townlands, Gortdearg (Red Field) and Gort na gCeann (Field of the Heads).

The great old Celtic feast of Bealtaine – May Day – was observed in the City in living memory. People made 'rounds' of varying degrees of complexity, reciting Christian prayers of atonement and supplication, but the other aspects of the pilgrimage – the merriment, dancing and drinking associated with the 'pattern day' and the leaving of money or pieces of cloth tied to bushes or trees in the City money or pieces of cloth – suggests a ritual far older than Christianity. Seanchaí Éamon Kelly, who grew up near this area, best conveys the devotion and the superstitions associated with it:

> Seven Our Fathers and seven Hail Marys and we are inside the wall, where we come to the mound, about the ninth station. You make the sign of the Cross here too, and on either side from the circular motion of the prayer pebble there are two hollows, like the inside of a basin, worn deep into the rock. There's a perfect circle cut into a flag over at the City.

Whatever that signifies?. You can be sure
it wasn't ratified by the Council of Trent.
On that mound you'd leave a token. A
safety pin, a hairpin, a button off your
clothes. It would have to be from your
person, a nail you'd have in your pocket,
a match, a piece of rosary beads, a holy
medal or a wingnut off your bicycle.
You'd see every class of a thing there. I
saw a sparking plug, a child's nipple, a
man's tie, a woman's garter, a hurley stick
and a crutch, all together in the one
place!

The men and women'd tear strips out
of the lining of their clothes, or pull a
thread out of a ravelling *gansey*, and the
girls'd take ribbons out of their hair and
tie 'em to the branches of the tree at the
holy well. When the pattern'd be over
that tree'd be festooned with *giobals*,
pennies and ha'pennies driven into the
bark, and a load of crutches there – if you
broke 'em up they'd keep you in firing for
a week. For there were cures!

There are hundreds of such holy wells in Ireland which were still places of devotion no more than a generation ago. There may even be a residual element of pilgrimage attached to some of them still. Although some of the sites are associated with a local early Christian saint, it is certain that the cult of these wells and the 'pattern' day – a particular date in the year, be it May Day, Midsummer or a date in between – when a combination of devotion, commerce, in the form of pedlars and fortune-hunters, and frolic, drinking and carousing took place, are vestiges of a pagan cult. The Celts regarded wells as sacred, not just because they contained water but because, being underground, they formed a link between the natural world and the Other-world. To look into a well is to look into the depths of the soul.

The four great Celtic festivals, all of which have survived in some form or another until our own time, were St Brigid's Eve (Imbolg), the first of spring; May Eve or Bealtaine, which marked the beginning of summer; St John's Eve, Midsummer's Eve, and Samhain or Hallowe'en, the beginning of winter and the festival of the dead, the spirits and the Underworld. Lesser festivals included Lughnasa, a fertility festival, the feast of the pagan god Lugh, and the winter solstice.

All these great feasts have survived precisely because they were Christianised by being linked with a suitable Christian feast. Imbolg became associated with the Celtic saint (or pagan goddess) Brigid, and Midsummer with the Feast Day of St John. (Bonfires are still lit on Midsummer's Eve.) St Brigid's Day was marked by wandering groups of 'Biddys' or 'Biddy-Boys' who visited the houses in the locality and performed songs or dances for the householders. Bealtaine is the 'pattern' day at many holy wells, and the fertility feast of Lughnasa, although perhaps less widely known, celebrates the plenitude of the harvest.

In his magnificent and justly famous play *Dancing at Lughnasa,* Irish playwright Brian Friel makes use of the pagan symbolism of the fertility festival to point up the tensions between conventional Chrisianity and paganism and ultimately to assert that there is no real difference between people, no matter what their belief system is.

Samhain, or Hallowe'en, has been a great winter festival for thousands of years, long before the current commercialisation of the date. The Celts believed that on that night, the veil between the natural world and the Otherworld, the world of the dead, was torn, and that spirits could move freely between their former home and their supernatural one. Christianity has effectively colonised this feast by dedicating the month of November to the memory of the souls of the dead: 1 November is All Saints' Day; 2 November All Souls' Day.

Apart from the observance of Samhain, when it was believed that spirits walked the earth, many of the customs associated with death, wakes and burials practised in Ireland within living memory had more to do with Celtic paganism than with Christianity and certainly had their roots in the ancient past. Kevin Danaher's *In Ireland Long Ago* gives an account of some of these customs: the drinking, the taking of snuff and the amusements people used to pass the time during the long hours or days of the wake, as it was essential that the body should never be left alone between death and burial.

It was customary, too, that at least some of the clothes of the dead person were given away to the poor. It was fairly usual that a relative or friend of the dead wore a suit of his clothes to Mass on the three Sundays following the funeral, and there are places where the new suit was specially made for the purpose, with the belief and intention that the dead man would, thereby, be properly clothed in the next world.

Danaher also gives an account of the custom of keening, or singing a *caoineadh* or lament over the dead body. Eugene O'Currry, in *Manners and Customs of the Ancient Irish*, describes such a lament, given by a young man for his brother, who had been killed by a fall from a horse:

He first recounted his genealogy, eulogised the spotless honour of his family, described in the tones of a sweet lullaby his chldhood and boyhood, then, changing the air suddenly, he spoke of his wrestling and hurling, his skill at plough-

ing, his horsemanship, his prowess at a
fight in a fair, his wooing and marriage,
and ended by suddenly bursting into a
loud, piercing but exquisitely beautiful
wail, which was again and again taken up
by the bystanders.

The *caoineadh* was not always a spontaneous
outpouring of grief by a loved one of the
deceased but sometimes a stylised ritual performed by a woman or group of women who
were expert in the activity. These women were
highly respected for the practice of this ancient
art and were rewarded with snuff and whiskey,
or sometimes even hired and paid for doing this
job.

The *caoineadh* as an art form found its
highest expression in the eighteenth century
poem 'Caoineadh Airt Uí Laoghaire', which was
composed by the dead man's widow, Eibhlín
Dubh Ní Chonaill, and which, despite its literary
qualities, contains the motifs and structure of a
traditional lament. A very famous Christian version
of a *caoineadh*, the passion song 'Caoineadh na
dTrí Mhuire', exists in many different versions all
over Ireland – another example of the grafting

of Christianity on to pagan customs. It shares with the keening of ordinary people the chorus line 'Ochón agus Ochón Ó', which might ordinarily occur something like this (quoted in *In Ireland Long Ago*):

O father, you have left! Ochón!
Why did you leave us? Ochón!
Or what did we do to you? Ochón!
That you went away from us? Ochón!
'Tis you that had plenty! Ochón!
And why did you leave us? Ochón!
Ochón! Ochón! Ullagón O!
Strong was your arm! Ochón!
Light was your step! Ochón!
Skilled were your hands! Ochón!
Poor are we without you! Ochón!
And why did you leave us? Ochón!
Ochón! Ochón! Ullagón O!

Keening was again and again denounced by synods of bishops and individual clergy as 'un-Christian'.

The wake games or amusements, which are described in detail in Seán Ó Súilleabháin's *Irish*

Wake Amusements and which included 'contests in strength, agility, dexterity . . . and athletics', were even more likely to arouse the ire of the clergy. Bishops and priests preached against them, especially in the nineteenth and early twentieth century, as being pagan and disrespectful. But it is certain that the rituals associated with wakes and funerals in Ireland were based on ancient customs and beliefs in the fluidity of the boundary between the natural world and the hereafter.

Drinking at wakes was an essential part of the proceedings (whiskey was the normal drink, as there were very many distilleries in Ireland in previous centuries) and Church leaders repeatedly inveighed against this custom. For instance, as late as 1903, Dr Hoare, Bishop of Ardagh and Clonmacnoise, issued a notice, which was to be displayed in all churches, forbidding, under pain of mortal sin, the drinking of alcohol at wakes and funerals.

Rituals, games and even the alcohol, snuff and tobacco consumed at the wakes had a therapeutic effect on the bereaved: the rituals were so unvarying and the participation of neighbours and community so unstinting during the several days and nights of the funeral process that the bereaved were given the opportunity both to grieve and to be comforted. Of recent years, with the decline of these customs in rural as well as urban areas, it is clear that contemporary strategies for dealing with bereavement – they can no longer be called rituals – are giving to the bereaved neither the comfort of family ritual nor the luxury of extended grieving.

The respect in which the Irish traditionally held their dead is evidenced by the great burial mounds of Newgrange, Knowth and Dowth in the Boyne Valley and the huge dolmens or cromlechs that are dotted around the country and that people still refer to as 'Diarmuid and Grainne's Bed', after the story of the fugitive lovers from the *Fiannaíocht*. This respect – and the rituals associated with it – held until the late twentieth century, when modern life and technology finally overcame the ancient customs that had survived despite the passing of many centuries.

8

CELTIC ECHOES

In a collection of essays called *The Celts*, edited by Joseph Raftery and published in 1964, Myles Dillon contributes a piece on 'Celtic Religion and Celtic Society':

> It is important to reflect, at the outset, that we must not think in terms of the great world religions, of our own Christian faith with its philosophy and theology and a highly developed ethical and moral doctrine, of which the ideal of charity is the perfect expression. Not even of the Mohammedanism which owes so much to the Old Testament, nor of Hinduism or the nobler Buddhist form of Indian religion. We are dealing here with primitive magic, for which modern analogies would most

readily be found in Africa or among the hill tribes of India or the still-pagan tribes of North America; although the general culture of the Celts in Gaul was higher than that statement implies, judged by their achievement in decorative art.

More than thirty years later, no Irish historian, commentator or cleric would say in public (whatever about in private) that Celtic spirituality is nothing more than 'primitive magic'. Celtic spirituality has come of age: it is now seen as being compatible with Christianity, if both are interpreted correctly. Furthermore, it is believed that Celtic spirituality can enrich the spiritual life of the thoughtful Christian.

The thirty-six years between 1964 and the end of the twentieth century have also seen in Ireland an unprecedented rejection of conventional Catholicism because of changes in society, liberalisation of legislation regarding moral and sexual matters and the disrepute that a small number of clergy and religious have brought upon the Church as a whole. It is no accident that the rise in interest in matters Celtic has coincided with this disillusionment. There is much that is appealing in the religion or world-view of the Celts (for we do not really know all that much in detail about the religion they practised and might not want to know about some its more unsavoury aspects), especially in a world threatened by ecological disaster, the breakdown of family and community bonds and the rise of materialism as an alternative religion.

Among the key texts of the new Celtic spirituality is John O'Donohue's *Anam Cara*. *Anam Cara* ('soul-friend', in Irish), has been enormously successful and hugely influential since it was published in 1997. It is both a powerful and poetic personal testament and a beautiful evocation of a kind of spirituality not of our time but which could be made relevant to our time. O'Donohoe, who was himself ordained as a Catholic priest or, as he says, 'druid' (he makes explicit the continuity of pagan and Christian religion in Ireland) com-bines in his books philosophical depth, poetic vision and, as the subtitle of *Anam Cara* empha-sises, *Spiritual Wisdom from the Celtic World*. It is a potent mix. O'Donohue himself consciously addresses the hunger for meaning of post-Christian, materialist man and his longing to belong to some community of grace. *Anam Cara* must be addressed becaue it is *the* important popular work of our age when it comes to the interpretation of the meaning of Celtic spirituality and its significance for twenty-first-century man.

In *Anam Cara*, O'Donohue attributes to the Celtic mindset the wisdom that recognises and accepts Eros (the opposite of the repressive Catholic mindset described in Chapter 6); that adores light and darkness with no sense of the superiority of one over the other; that is in tune with the rhythm of the day, the year and the life of man; that believes in the 'primordial innocence' of the body and completely lacks the sense of body-soul dualism that early Christianity absorbed from the Greeks; that regards animals as possessing an eternal truth; that values the circle and the spiral as a 'negative capability' (Keats's theory that we should be content to be in a state of doubt and mystery 'without any irritable reaching after fact and reason'); that sees itself as being connected to the land in a numinous way; and that knows that the eternal world is close to the natural world, so that death is not such a long journey.

An interesting observation made by O'Donohue is that 'the light in Celtic consciousness is a penumbral light', and he points out that the two traditions of silence and speech find full expression in the Celtic tradition. The early Christian monks denied themselves speech but preserved, by writing them down, stories such as the *Táin* that had come down for generations in the oral tradition. Thus they respected the past and the collective memory of the race, even as they themselves worshipped another God.

John O'Donohue, himself a poet, comments on the language of the Celts as 'a language of lyrical and reverential observation' rather than a discursive one.

In other words, the Celts have much to teach us. By looking back to and absorbing a belief system that was practised by our ancestors and is in keeping with the topography and traditions of the country, we can experience a more real and harmonious spiritual life – or so the theory suggests.

Philosopher John Moriarty in his essay 'The Blackbird and the Bell: Reflections on the Celtic Tradition', in the collection *Celtic Threads,* warns, with jusification, against having too sunny an image of the Celtic tradition. There is 'at least as much darkness in the Celtic tradition as there is light', he says. Moriarty mentions the relics of the Celtic darkness that have survived until our time, especially the use of the evil eye and *piseoga*, many of them negative or destructive. *Celtic Threads* is an interesting and valuable collection, the justification for which, the editor Padraigín Clancy tell us, is that: 'As we look to the future, Celtic spirituality may offer us a certain refuge that is not only revitalising but necessary.'

Celtic spirituality has, therefore, survived: it is intertwined with our interpretation of Christianity; it still manifests itself in rituals that predate Christianity. Most of all, it seems that it exists as a kind of substratum of consciousness, as a collective memory of a spirituality that was more holistic and respectful of the world, both natural and supernatural.

SELECT BIBLIOGRAPHY

Clancy, Padraigín. *Celtic Threads: Exploring the Wisdom of Our Heritage*. Dublin: Veritas Publications, 1999.

Cross, Eric. *The Tailor and Ansty*. Dublin and Cork: Mercier Press, 1964.

Dames, Michael. *Mythic Ireland*. London: Thames and Hudson, 1992.

De Paor, Liam. *Saint Patrick's World*. Dublin: Four Courts Press, 1993.

Danaher, Kevin. *Folktales from the Irish Countryside*. Dublin and Cork: Mercier Press, 1967.

——————. *In Ireland Long Ago*. Dublin and Cork: Mercier Press, 1964.

——————. *The Year in Ireland: Irish Calendar Customs*. Dublin and Cork: Mercier Press, 1972.

Dillon, Myles, ed. *Irish Sagas*. Dublin and Cork: Mercier Press, 1968.

Hickey, Donal. *Stone Mad for Music: the Sliabh Luachra Story*. Dublin: Marino Books, 1999.

Kavanagh, P. J. *Voices in Ireland: A Traveller's Literary Companion*. London: John Murray, 1994.

Lehane, Brendan. *Early Celtic Christianity*. London: John Murray, 1968.

Mac Cana, Pronsias. *Celtic Mythology*. Middlesex: Newnes Books, 1968.

McMahon, Sean. *A Short History of Ireland*. Dublin and Cork: Mercier Press, 1996.

—————. *A Little Book of Celtic Wisdom*. Belfast: Appletree Press, 1995.

—————. *The Island of Saints and Scholars*. Dublin and Cork: Mercier Press, 2001.

————— and Jo O'Donoghue, eds. *Taisce Duan*. Swords, County Dublin: Poolbeg Press, 1992.

Mahon, Bríd. *Irish Folklore*. Dublin and Cork: Mercier Press, 2000.

Meyer, Kuno. *Selections from Ancient Irish Poetry*. London: Constable, 1959.

Neeson, Eoin. *Celtic Myths and Legends*. Dublin and Cork: Mercier Press, 1998.

O'Curry, Eugene. *Manners and Customs of the Ancient Irish*. London, 1873.

O'Donohue, John. *Anam Cara: Spiritual Wisdom from the Celtic World*. London: Bantam Press, 1997.

—————. *Eternal Echoes: Exploring Our Hunger to Belong*. London: Bantam Press, 1998.

Ó Duinn, Seán, OSB. *Where Three Streams Meet: Celtic Spirituality*. Dublin: The Columba Press, 2000.

Ó Súilleabháin, Seán. *Irish Wake Amusements*. Dublin and Cork: Mercier Press, 1967.

Raftery, Joseph, ed. *The Celts*. Dublin and Cork: Mercier Press, 1964.

Walsh, John R. and Thomas Bradley, *A History of the Irish Church 400–700 AD*. Dublin: The Columba Press, 1991.

Whiteside, Lesley. *The Spirituality of Saint Patrick*. Dublin: The Columba Press, 1996.